FAITH INTERRUPTED

A JOURNEY TO THE END OF FAITH AND BACK AGAIN

Amy Marsh DeMasters

Dr. Dave DeMasters

FAITH INTERRUPTED

Scripture References:

Unless otherwise noted, all Scripture references are taken from the Holy Bible, New International Version
Scripture references marked ESV are taken from The English Standard Version
Scripture references marked KJV are taken from The King James Version

Copyright 2016 by Amy Marsh DeMasters
and Dr. Dave DeMasters
All Rights Reserved
This book may not be reproduced in whole or in part, by any means, without written permission of the author.
ISBN-13: 978-0692771983
ISBN-10: 0692771980

Printed by CreateSpace, an Amazon.com Company

FAITH INTERRUPTED

FAITH INTERRUPTED

A JOURNEY TO THE END OF FAITH AND BACK AGAIN

Amy Marsh DeMasters

Dr. Dave DeMasters

FAITH INTERRUPTED

Dedication

To Josh and Chelsea—

Together we can dance in the storms!

FAITH INTERRUPTED

A Special Thank You

...to those who helped us along our journey back from the end of our faith...

- **DD Uthe**... it's hard to put words to what you did...this went WAY BEYOND payback, sis!
- **Jeff Uthe**... you came with a life boat, and let us sail with you for a looong time!
- **Pastor Shane & Sue Schlesman (West End Assembly of God, Richmond, VA)**...to our best friends in life...for the gift of your unwavering love
- **Mom & Dad Marsh**...bailing us out and standing strong beside us.
- **Mom DeMasters**...for being a rock in the moment of crisis, and that kitchen renovation at just the right time.
- **Don & Barbara Benton**...for jobs, support and hope, right when we needed it most.
- **Pastor Kerry Shook and Woodlands Church (The Woodlands, TX)**...for being a safe place to land and get our bearings.
- **Jodi Oehike (BackPacker Church)**...you woke up our spirits with the Spirit of God.
- **Donna Blackman**...you were grace straight from heaven to work with me on "Chocolate" for $20 at a time
- **Pastor John & Kelly Sherrill and Declaration Church (Spring, TX)**...you welcomed us home!

FAITH INTERRUPTED

FAITH INTERRUPTED

CONTENTS

DEDICATION
PRELUDE
INTRODUCTION

THE SHOCK
1. Faith Interrupted
2. I Want to Run
3. If I Could Pray
4. We Used to Dance
5. Pieces of My Brokenness
6. Beautiful Basket
7. What's Really Going On?
8. Canyon's Edge

THE STRUGGLE
9. Some Kind of Faith
10. Life Comes at You Sideways
11. Raw God
12. The Stuff of Me
13. Disconnected
14. When Vanity Makes Sense

THE SURVIVING
15. Moment of Surprise!
16. I Choose to Dance
17. Child in Heart
18. Dirty Hands and Skinned Knees

CONCLUSION

FAITH INTERRUPTED

Prelude-Dave

Not long ago we experienced the most devastating trauma of our lives to that point. It knocked us down, it knocked us out, and it changed everything about our lives. At that time, Amy wrote explicitly about the experience...what she felt, what she thought, what she feared.

Faith Interrupted contains eighteen of these powerful journal entries. They are straightforward, they are emotional, and they are real. Amy then recounts the emotional context of each journal entry, sharing what led to it, or what she was thinking at the time. This provides you with a greater understanding of the entry, and allows you to personally connect it to your own life.

I conclude each chapter with a spiritual and psychological analysis to provide a frame of reference for what is taking place.

The book progresses through three phases:

FAITH INTERRUPTED

In *Part One – The Shock*, the entries are visceral, conveying the absolute reality of the devastation. You will find comfort in the fact that you are not alone in the pain you feel, or the thoughts that stab your mind.

In *Part Two – The Struggle*, the book recounts that season where the mind attempts to reconcile experiences and belief. You will identify with the great gulf that seems fixed between the two, and the bridge that spans the gap.

In *Part Three – The Surviving*, we explain the emergence of a new post-trauma person, one who is marked by the past, but not trapped by it.

Faith Interrupted is a flashlight for those who have experienced a trauma that pushed them beyond the edge of their faith, and into the darkness of the unknown. It is a companion, assuring them they are not alone, and that they are not forgotten. Ultimately it serves as a trail-guide to illuminate a way back to the God who was hidden along the way.

FAITH INTERRUPTED

Introduction-Amy

We are struck down in our lives. We are forced to endure things we never anticipated. It may be financial destruction, emotional heartache, or physical suffering. Each of us has our own path to walk. You may have faced excruciating, overwhelming obstacles. But, it is not about what we face externally that shapes us—and that is not what we address on these pages. *Faith Interrupted* is about understanding the inner struggle in the midst of those outer challenges. It is about the seemingly contradictory paradox of disbelief and faith. It is about the personal challenge to survive, and maybe even grow, on such a journey. It is about what we think we know in the midst of what we don't know.

My faith was interrupted. Everything changed in a matter of days as the result of an unexpected, traumatic event. Within a matter of weeks we lost our home, our income, and our livelihood. We lost our friends. We drove to Texas with just a few suitcases, moved in with family, and started over. I now woke up in a different home...in a different world, really. We struggled to find jobs in the recession. Our kids were thrown into new schools. We had no money, and seemingly no way to make it. All the while I spun in confusion as to what had happened and what we could have done to prevent the series of events that brought us here.

I knew God was with us in the big decisions...but I lost Him after that. I felt alone and deeply afraid of what would come next. I felt paralyzed—unable to move forward. I went from talking to God every day to a state of absolute shock—unable to grasp what had happened weeks before...and unable to hold on to God.

I wrote about my inner conflict in a journal. I still have that journal, and those words provide the backbone of this book. They are a glimpse into my heart when I wanted to shut down and hide. By interacting with these writings and then hearing my thoughts of reflection, I hope you can identify with the pain and maybe catch a glimpse of a larger context. I warn you, some of these are dark. It was dark inside my soul for a while.

Walking with me through this struggle was my dear husband, Dave. He had his own battles to fight as well as fighting for me and our kids, Josh and Chelsea. But, he held my hand and we walked together. Beyond being my soul mate and my deepest love in this life, he was (and is) my counselor, my pastor, and my very best friend. He cares for my soul like no one in this world ever could. So, along with my thoughts and feelings, Dave will share his perspective as the counselor/pastor guiding us through a difficult journey of faith. His insights are priceless to me. He is the earthly reason I am alive and well--very well --today. I urge you to listen to him on these pages. He has the wisdom to help us move forward.

It is our prayer that these pages will help you to understand your own pain, will guide you to a better understanding of your own faith, and will walk you down a more clear path to hold onto God in the midst of whatever you are going through.

FAITH INTERRUPTED

PART 1:
THE SHOCK

FAITH INTERRUPTED

1
Faith Interrupted

Journal Excerpt:

Like a river, the waters of my faith have suddenly been stopped and the riverbed is dry and barren.

Everything was gone in one terrible moment.

My body has yet to find the place my soul fled to. I used to believe everything happened for a reason. Now nothing has reason. I no longer want to change the world through my life. I no longer want to show people the way to God. I do not understand God myself. My truth is now only what I am experiencing. Everyone lives and dies. Everyone finds happiness and endures pain...it is just life. And we survive...at least I think we do.

How odd to find myself in this place of interrupted faith after decades of walking with God. I feel somehow disconnected from that person. How strange it will be if I spend the second half of my life without my faith—without a deeper meaning to life. It does feel quite empty to live this way. I am bored in a book without pictures, but I don't know how to change that.

In a moment—in one breath--I lost myself. I am disoriented, confused, fighting depression and hopelessness.

My faith—the force that has guided my life up till now—has been interrupted.

I wonder if the waters will wash back over me...

Amy's Thoughts:

For more than twenty years I was busy crusading for a cause! I loved it. It was who I was. It was what I did. Because I could fight, I did. I knew that the victories came from God, and I relished the adventure with God and with my family. I lived with passion and was always on a mission of some sort.

But, that all changed.

Now, I didn't have the strength or will to go on. I felt dead inside. I was broken and wounded...crushed really.

My faith was no longer a sword I could wield. My faith was just a carcass.

I suddenly found myself in a place where I could not fight. I could not change my circumstances or even find within the courage to push forward.

So, because I couldn't do anything else, I waited.

FAITH INTERRUPTED

Dr. Dave's Counsel:

We will all experience this at some point...seeming abandonment by God. We can be cruising along in our life, flush with power, strong in our belief, charging every hill, with absolute confidence in our God, ourselves, and our victory. Right up until it is gone. Those moments are human. Those moments are real. Jesus himself faced that moment when He cried out:

> *"My God, My God, Why have you forsaken me?"*
> (Matthew 27:46).

No matter what your theological view of what is occurring there, it is clear that Jesus was dealing with seemingly insurmountable feelings of abandonment. If He can face that, so can we.

What is the response to that? How do we deal with it? There are two answers. The first is this...**God is a big boy.** He can take whatever we can dish out. There are definitely times when we need to let the pain out, honestly, directly, and maybe even forcefully, to God. You see, God is omniscient--He knows everything. That means He already knows the pain that you are experiencing. So it's ok to tell Him about it yourself. When we read the words of Jesus from Matthew 27:46, I can picture Jesus screaming those words. I can hear the

FAITH INTERRUPTED

pain and fear in His voice. It may not have happened that way, but I can identify with it if it did. And that's the point for me...God can take whatever I can dish out. And sometimes it is VERY GOOD for me to dish out my feelings in a very honest way. Because then I learn that He doesn't run away. He doesn't abandon me. He doesn't flee. He doesn't strike me back for being angry with Him. He remains steadfast. Because God is a big boy, He can take it.

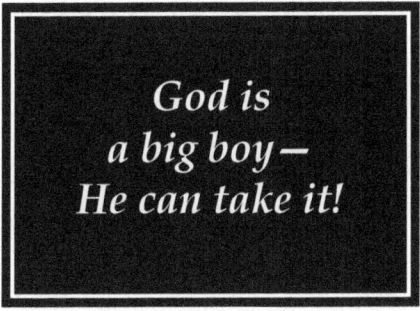

God is a big boy — He can take it!

The second response is from the opposite end of the emotional spectrum. God has given us a direct promise in this instance. No matter how deep those feelings may run, or how overwhelmed I may feel. Jesus makes me a promise:

> *"I will not leave you as orphans ...*
> *I will come to you"* (John 14:18).

He is ... ON HIS WAY TO ME. That's what I take from that verse. My Dad, who is bigger than anyone else's dad, is on His way to me. The wording here is interesting. He doesn't say that He will not leave us

"AN orphan." He says that He will not leave us "AS orphans." There is a huge difference in those two statements. An orphan has no father. He is completely fatherless. There is no parent for an orphan. He is all-alone. But God is our Father. I am His son. You are His son or daughter. Although it may feel like we are orphans, once we have become a follower of Christ, we are NEVER, NEVER an orphan again.

My faith foundation is that He is my Father and I am His son. I am not an orphan; I have a Dad. I am not alone; I am a son. Upon that foundation I can build the second truth that My Father is on His way. He has heard my cry and He is coming. He has seen my situation and is headed to me. And once He gets here it will be alright.

Now…I'm not making a promise as to WHEN He is going to come. He doesn't tell us that. But often it is enough that He knows what is going on, and He is…

ON

HIS

WAY!

2
I Want to Run

Journal Excerpt:

I want to run away...from me
But who knows where I am?
Who knows my heart and who can carry me?
If I run, will I be forever lost?
God, would You find me?
God, does it even matter?

I want to run away...from me
Turn my back and keep on moving
But I am held in place by the chords of my life
All its fingers holding on to me
With a steel grip I cannot escape.

Amy's Thoughts:

I wanted to run away from my life. I wanted to flee from the depression that was boxing me in. But there was nowhere to go and nothing I could do that would change the feelings inside me.

The instinct to run was palpable every morning as I woke up. When the sleeping fog lifted and the reality of my life sunk in, the pain would return...and then the fear. And then I would want to run away again. But I was also afraid of what running would lead to. There was nowhere to run that would take away the pain in my heart.

Psalm 55:6-8 says, *"oh, that I had the wings of a dove! I would fly away and be at rest – I would flee far away and stay in the desert; I would hurry to my place of shelter far from the tempest and storm."*

I wanted to run, but in the midst of these fears, I could feel my family—my husband, my son, my daughter, my mom and my dad--holding me in place. Like ropes tying a boat to shore, they held on to me. These were my "chords of life." They kept me from drifting away. Their presence provided a familiar, well-worn track to walk on. I was changed and I was broken, but I found the way to move forward because of them. They held my

FAITH INTERRUPTED

hand, they walked beside me. And even without words they led me by being there.

Through all the changes and challenges of many years, Dave and I have worked at our marriage. We made sure difficulties and disagreements drove us together, not apart. We sacrificed to ensure our family was strong and the bond was tight. Sometimes we let our dreams go. We gave up being "right" many times. We lived for one another at the expense of those around us. You will always have to choose your priorities and live in light of them.

We chose each other. We poured the strength of ourselves into one another. Through the years, we wove together a strong rope of intertwined hearts. That rope held me as I struggled and fell. That rope held me when I couldn't hold on myself. That rope held me when I gave up.

I remember being surprised that so much was wrong, but our family was still strong. So much was lost, yet the core of US was good. So much pain was there, but in the midst of that pain I was held by my family. They were the cords holding on to me and keeping me safe.

Dr. Dave's Counsel:

The issue at hand is contra-intuitive. Let me start with the intuitive part. The gut reaction (natural instinct) we have in trauma is to RUN! The feelings described in this chapter are right on the verge of panic, and at times across the line into full blown fear. If you could run you would, but you know that you can't outrun those feelings. Like Jonah, once you had run as far and as fast as you could run, when you looked up, that pain and depression would be there waiting on you...almost as if it knew where you were going. That's the intuitive part.

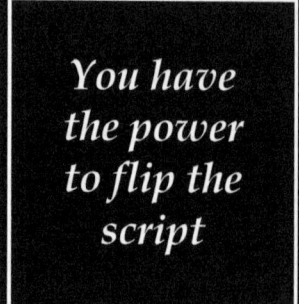

You have the power to flip the script

Now for the contra: the word is the shortened version of "contradict" – meaning the opposite. So we do the opposite. We think the opposite. Instead of viewing the depression (or whatever negative emotion is chasing you) as omnipresent, we flip it and realize that it is God, in His comfort that is there. Though He isn't "fixing it," He is "feeling it" and wants to feel it with us. Don't run FROM the depression. Instead, stand there in it and fully fix your heart, your mind, and your emotions on Him.

FAITH INTERRUPTED

Consider Psalm 139 from that perspective. This text is normally presented in light of those who want to run from God (like Jonah) and demonstrate that God is everywhere you want to run (as I described above). But read the passage "contra"...read it in the opposite, that HE is there in everything I face, in every hurt, in every situation. He is THERE with me! I'll put in some thoughts in parenthesis to help (v 7-10).

"Where can I go (that you are not) from your Spirit? Where can I flee from your presence?
If I go up to the heavens, you are there (with me); if I make my bed in the depths, you are there (with me).
If I rise on the wings of the dawn (you are there with me), if I settle on the far side of the sea (you are there with me),
Even there your hand will guide me, (even there) your right hand will hold me fast."

So don't run. Stay. As hard as it is, stay in the emotion and bring Jesus into it with you ... because He is there. You are not alone. You are not abandoned. Our fear is that the emotion will overwhelm and overpower us. The only way to overcome that fear (short of pharmaceuticals☺) is to stay in it and allow God to meet it, to take it, and to love you through it.

Now, there is a line out there where emotions can take completely over. You know when that is happening, and I do NOT recommend that you face that kind of power alone. You must have the support of a friend or a counselor who can make sure you are safe, to walk with you through it. These are deep waters, and sometimes people drown in deep waters. I am not recommending that.

What I am recommending is to recognize that **you have the power to flip the script**, and to redefine your emotional orientation. Instead of seeing the depression as your master, see Him as the master of your depression. Though the jar may be half empty, or three-quarters empty, or there is only a drop of hope in the jar, recognize the power of that one, single, drop – and focus on that!

3
If I Could Pray

Journal Excerpt:

If I could pray, I would ask for a life again.
I would ask for the terrible fear that rises inside of me, choking me, to be laid to rest.
If I could pray.

Sometimes we just cannot bring our fragile hearts to the place of prayer. Cannot let down the paper-thin layer that so carefully protects us and speak—heart to heart—with our Creator. That delicate layer of clothing is the only thing between us and nakedness.

We cling to the covering—not out of pride—for that thick coat was shed long ago. This final transparent gown is all that stands between me and an unknown, dark place of the soul.

I still cannot pray. Not because of what happened--the pain has lessened over time.

It is the uncertainty of what could happen next that wrestles with the worst I can imagine.

My mind tries to formulate the next step, but my heart knows the ground is crumbling beneath my feet.

I cannot move...cannot process or advance.

If I could pray, if I could bear my nakedness to the One who knows me...
I would ask to be rescued before it is too late.
I would ask for what makes my humanity to be restored.
I would ask for a way to live again.
I would ask for hope...if I could pray.

FAITH INTERRUPTED

Amy's Thoughts:

Sometimes we are in such a low and vulnerable place that we are without words and find ourselves unable to reach out to pray. I can remember the uncertainty I felt as I wrote the words above. I remember the confusion as well.

All I could find within myself was a faint desire...a weak strength...just enough to reach in the right direction. In the middle of my pain, I thought my faith was gone. I felt numb. I felt broken. I had lost my sense of confidence in who God was and who I was. I had only a weak desire to pray... if I could.

But I couldn't.

I couldn't form the words to ask God for help. I didn't know what to pray or how to pray. It was like my mind was stuck in quick sand. I was being pulled under, and unable to stop it. I couldn't even cry out to be rescued.

Dr. Dave's Counsel:

If I Could Pray comes from a place that is almost visceral in its power. It is like those times in your life when the emotion is so intense that you cannot articulate words, and all you want to do is SCREAM. And sometimes we do. Those unintelligible sounds, however guttural they may be, convey a ton of meaning…sometimes more than a thousand carefully crafted words by the most articulate poet. These are the moments I am so thankful to be in a relationship with an omniscient God—a God who knows absolutely everything.

> *I didn't just show up on His radar screen because I am emotionally red-lining…*

1 John 3:20 says, "*For whenever our heart condemns us, God is greater than our heart, and he knows everything*" (ESV).

He knows my pain. He knows the intensity of my pain. He knows that the pain is so strong that I can't put words to it. He even knows the meaning of the scream.

He knows.

FAITH INTERRUPTED

On the practical side, that means that He is not surprised by what I'm feeling or thinking. He didn't wake up this morning and suddenly become aware of me. He never says "Hey angels, let's check in on Dave and see what's going on with him." One of my seminary professors once said to me, "God pays as much attention to you as if you were the only being in existence other than Him." I didn't just show up on His radar screen because I am emotionally red-lining in anger, fear, depression, and loneliness. No. He has intimately known my every thought.
My every feeling...

He knows.

This takes on a second meaning. He not only knows it all intellectually (knows that it is happening), He also knows it experientially with us.

Hebrews 4:15 says, *"For we do not have a High priest who is unable to sympathize with our weaknesses, but we have one who has been tempted in every way, just as we are – yet was without sin."*

Double negatives are tough, and we have one here (*do not, unable*). In math, that means we can eliminate them both as they cancel each other out. In literature it is the same. So this means we HAVE a High Priest who HAS been touched with the feeling of our infirmity! He feels what we feel. He has experienced what we experience.

FAITH INTERRUPTED

Jesus faced excruciating circumstances in His life: the betrayal of a close friend, the death of someone He loved. If fact, at one point Luke 22:44 states that Jesus experienced such emotional pain that He was sweating like great drops of blood (called *hematohidrosis*). That's emotional pressure I have never known, and hardly understand. And then, of course, He was crucified, after being whipped 39 times by a whip with bone spurs on the end. He gets it. He is here. He is engaged.

Though He may be silent at the moment...

He knows.

4
We Used to Dance

Journal Excerpt:

I cannot see Him.

But I remember what He is like. I remember His voice and so I wonder if I will hear it once again.

I remember the sense of His touch, and I hope His hand will find mine again one day.

He and I used to see the world through each other's eyes. He is completely gone now, and I miss the view.

I miss the light and the sparkles He gave me.

Colors are so dull without Him. The trees are silent and the stars don't sing when He is gone.

We used to dance.

Is that a memory or just a dream? I catch a glimpse now and then, when He passes by. The light brush against my cheek causes me to turn toward...nothing. Soft words float by like a quiet breeze, but I feel them. However faint, these things are real and they fill me with faded memories of beauty and peace.

I'm pretty sure...we used to dance.

FAITH INTERRUPTED

Amy's Thoughts:

This is the saddest journal entry for me. Psalms 42:1ff mirrors my thoughts here:

"My soul thirsts for God, for the living God. When can I go and meet with God? My tears have been my food day and night, while men say to me all day long, 'Where is your God?' These things I remember as I pour out my soul: how I used to go with the multitude, leading the procession to the house of God, with shouts of joy and thanksgiving among the festive throng."

Dancing takes place when we have joy. There was no dancing now and wouldn't be for quite some time...for years, really. There was no bouncing back or recovery that I could sense. This was a quiet, barren winter for me. During those months, the memory of close communion with God haunted me. It broke my heart that I didn't feel it anymore, but I still remembered what I once had. I wondered if the dance would return, if my joy would return...if He would return.

Dr. Dave's Counsel:

This is a good time for a lesson on the brain. Memories develop in our brain as chemicals and electrical impulses track through the tissue in our cortex. The more frequently we visit that memory, or place in the brain (recall), the more deeply imbedded it becomes. If we do not visit that memory, it fades and eventually is lost.

For example, if I asked you what you had for dinner on June 14, 1995 you probably wouldn't remember. It was

> *What we think becomes the fabric of our memory landscape*

long ago and nothing significant to remember. But you might remember if June 14th was your birthday. And you might remember if on this particular birthday your parents threw a party for you and hired a clown for entertainment. You might remember more if the "clown experience" was fine until you posed for a picture while blowing out your candles and the clown beside you threw up all over your cake...on June 14, 1995. In this case you probably would remember that you DIDN'T have cake on that day. And you might remember the hamburgers on the grill that you almost threw-up yourself! In fact, you might not really care for clowns anymore, especially on your birthday.

You see, trauma is an explosion in the brain. It is a deep chemical and electrical experience. In revisiting a memory, which we often do, it becomes even more deeply ingrained. Because of their explosive nature, traumas actually have the unintended consequence of negatively impacting lesser memories, which then fade from our minds.

Of such can be our memories of God. We easily remember the trauma. It is well marked and frequently visited. Trauma can then become a solar eclipse on the good things that we easily remembered before, and become a magnet for our intellectual and emotional attention. We lose sight of the good, and become fixed on the bad, frequently compounding the experience. Eventually, this event seems to become its own black hole, sucking the life and light out of us.

It is here that psychology can help. We have learned that our attention span is limited to about 90 seconds. What that means is that in most cases, if we can endure a temptation for 90 seconds, it significantly loses its power in our lives. The more frequently I redirect my attention for those 90 seconds the LESS POWER is has over me. In my counseling practice I encourage people with anxiety and depressive tendencies with this truth:

FAITH INTERRUPTED

"YOU get to choose what you think about for the next 90 seconds. When temptation comes, you have control over what comes next."

God made us in His image with intellect, emotion and will. We get to make the decision about what we think – and **what we think becomes the fabric of our memory landscape, or memory-scape.** The more we choose the positive things, the more positive we become. We win the battle 90 seconds at a time.

Amy lost the memory of the dance, because her attention was distracted away from it. She eventually regained the dance, by fighting for the little bit she remembered, and then focusing on that. Eventually, she recovered those memories, and then recovered those practices, and could dance in the storm again. She won the battle…

90 seconds at a time.

5
Pieces of My Brokenness

Journal Excerpt:

With one rough thoughtless swing, hope is sent plummeting to the ground, smashed into a thousand pieces...yet again.

How many times can I find the strength within me to get down on my knees, gather up the remains, and repair them? What was once beautiful art hardly resembles its original form. ...Betrayed and broken, then slowly beginning to be restored...only to fall again...and again.

With each fall I wonder, "Am I at the final place of hopelessness?"

FAITH INTERRUPTED

I find myself sitting on the floor with broken rubble all around me. To my right I see a sparkling corner piece with the mystical dark sapphire still attached. I eagerly reach out to pick it up but it crumbles to powder in my hand. And I am left with one stone in the midst of grey dust.

Warm tears run down my face and gently land on the stone, making it sparkle like an evening rainfall.

What beauty has been lost!

FAITH INTERRUPTED

Amy's Thoughts:

I realized while I wrote these words that I had become stuck in a destructive cycle of looking at my past—looking at what I once had. I kept trying to figure out how I could have prevented the loss...and how I could get it all back. I tried to put the pieces back together. I would go over and over things in my mind—reliving those last days and trying to change the outcome. I would re-live the pain and feel each devastating blow again and again.

We cannot go back.

We will not always understand where things went wrong. We may never know the answers to the questions in our heart. If we are trying to solve a problem with no solution or if we are trying to piece together the dust and rubble, we just can't ever seem to do it. If we are not careful, we can become stuck in that place for months or even years.

When we look only at what we have lost, we are unable to move ahead. We condemn ourselves for our failures and shortcomings...as well as things out of our control. Trouble and pain do not necessarily come from our own sin and failure, but trouble and pain will eventually come. Yes, we generally reap what we sow. It is a truth of nature and the Bible that our actions and our life will bring back to us the kinds of things we put into it. But, sometimes things happen to bring about a seismic change in a life. Sometimes other people's choices put actions in motion that affect us.

In John 9 Jesus healed a blind man. The disciples ask Jesus if this man was blind because of his own sin or his parent's sin. They were sure that bad things happen to bad people and good things happen to good people, and that's the only way it works. Many of us think that way today. But, Jesus said the only reason he was blind was so God could perform this miracle in him—so people would see what God can do.

I had to come to terms with my own situation and realized that I didn't know why it happened, and I might never know. At that point I couldn't comprehend how God might be able to work through the circumstances. What I did realize is that good things can come from dust. God made mankind from dust. That was good. Perhaps there was something good that could come from this, too.

FAITH INTERRUPTED

Dr. Dave's Counsel:

Turning point.

In every situation there is a turning point...a moment in time when our attention shifts, our focus shifts...our heart shifts. Amy has described it in this chapter. The darkness is beginning to lift and we can see a little again. This is a powerful moment of change. It is when we realize, perhaps for the first time since the devastation, that there is a choice--we actually do have the power to choose. This is AWESOME. It's our very own Robert Frost moment in the midst of this season...

> *"Two roads diverged in a yellow wood...*
> *And I took the one less traveled by,*
> *And that has made all the difference"*

It is a tremendous victory to finally make it to the fork in the road! To finally be at a place where I can see that there is another option for me, that there is an off-ramp from this seemingly endless highway. This is a KEY MOMENT OF VICTORY. A moment I do not want us to miss. It is an opportunity to take your life back, and to move it in the direction of healing, hope and health. In this moment we break the chain that binds us and we move forward, perhaps for the first time in a long time, toward the life that God has been preparing us for. So we choose life.

Deuteronomy 30:19 says,

"Today I am giving you a choice of two ways. And I ask heaven and earth to be witnesses of your choice. You can choose life or death. The one choice will bring a blessing. The other choice will bring a curse. So choose life! Then you and your children will live" (ESV).

> *Where your thoughts go--
> everything follows*

Choices have ramifications. When we choose a path for our thoughts that leads toward life, more life springs forth. When we choose a path for our thoughts that leads toward death, more death follows. When I teach counseling and psychology students the inner dynamics of man, I boil it down pretty simply: "What you think about, you will eventually feel, and what you feel, you will eventually do. Where your thoughts go, everything follows." This verse summarizes that. We choose what our mind feasts upon. It can either be thoughts that lead to life, or thoughts that lead to death.

Thank God that you can have a "yellow wood" moment

FAITH INTERRUPTED

regarding your devastation. You know where the one road leads, and it isn't good. It's never good.

You are at a Y ...

Choose life!

FAITH INTERRUPTED

6
Beautiful Basket

Journal Excerpt:

We put pressure on ourselves
To be so much more than God intended us to be.
And, as a result, we become so much less.

Our hearts drag under the weight we have placed upon them

And we are never free...

...to just be beautiful.

Amy's Thoughts:

People shy away from weakness and failure. And yet any success we do find is tenuous at best. It is a falsity that only hurts us. One of the worst parts of dealing with my crisis in life and faith was the utter failure I felt. Professionally and personally I was inadequate. I found myself emotionally weak...well, I should be honest here...unstable would better describe it. I could not always contain my emotions. I found it difficult to function in a work environment, but I needed to work for the money. I was not the positive, encouraging, bubbly mom I had always been for my children. I lost some critical characteristics that made Amy...well, Amy. My husband lost some of the woman he had loved and married over 20 years before. I'm sure that scared him as much as it scared me.

My teenage daughter, Chelsea, began calling me a pet name during these years of struggle. I would...many times...breakdown crying in front of my teenage kids and would say, "I'm sorry I'm such a basket case!" My family was so loving and encouraging to me in those times. And Chelsea started to call me her **"beautiful basket."** That name has stuck. And the name always reminds me that God sees each of us as a beautiful child

FAITH INTERRUPTED

that He loves. And that in our weakness He can show us His strength.

My weakness is not "fixed" now. I'm not back to the way I used to be. I don't think I ever will be. So, I try to be open and honest about it. I hope that my weaknesses will showcase God's strength and people will see God in a new way because of my story.

FAITH INTERRUPTED

Dr. Dave's Counsel:

This chapter reveals a beautiful truth. Many times, if not most (honestly, if not all), our performance expectations are based on the perceptions of others. To say it another way, the perceptions of others become the demands of performance, which place pressure upon us. If we could just be free to admit to ourselves where we really are, and what we can really do, we would break the back of false performance and unspeakable pressure. If it isn't hard enough to function in the midst of desolation, our right-side brain processes what everyone else wants, and we become crushed under the weight of it all.

God sees each of us as a beautiful child

Psychologically, this is incredibly unhealthy. Our cognitive and emotional resources are needed to focus on and process our inner healing. When these are diverted to face external pressures, our healing is stunted, and we spend longer and longer times in pain.

Chelsea's validation of Amy's pain created a positive viewpoint of emerging beauty, and she became a

FAITH INTERRUPTED

beautiful basket. God speaks directly to this in Isaiah 61:3 (NSV)...

> "Beauty for ashes
> Joy for mourning and
> Praise for despair."

Generally speaking this is progressive, not instantaneous. God can work this miracle. I have seen it. But for me, and many like me, it is a process. In the midst of the ashes, He begins to bring forth a beauty. In the mist of mourning He begins to bring a joy. In the midst of despair He begins to bring forth praise. It may just be a whimper at first, but as He acknowledges, from an acorn comes

> "a mighty oak of righteousness that brings forth glory."

As hard as it is for us to understand, we become increasingly beautiful to God when we turn to Him in the flames of our trials and tribulations. When we turn our tear stained faces toward Him, He is drawn to us. He can't help Himself. He just has to love us.

I encourage you to see the beauty that you have developed, or are developing because of your struggle. Embrace that beauty. See yourself as the beloved son and daughter that you are.

You are...**a beautiful basket.**

FAITH INTERRUPTED

7
What's Really Going On?

Journal Excerpt:

These weak and shaking legs stand on a barren mountain top with only a mist of grey around them. The northern wind whips at my face, now streaked with tears of pain.

My naked arms are held outstretched before me...and I wonder why they are so empty.

Where has it gone?

My faith has been stolen, ripped from my arms in a moment. Who am I now without it?

FAITH INTERRUPTED

Am I still alive?

I chose to pursue God and seek a spiritual life. My choice IS my faith—seasons of life spent in prayer and meditation in an effort to understand God and myself. Half a lifetime given to sharing with others this God I thought I knew.

In those days the intense force of my life was driven by my faith. Were these decades of passion wasted?

What difference has it made that I pursued God? And why have I lived a life for others?

Suddenly, this faith that was part of me has been brutally attacked...like a child ripped away from his mother's arms. And I stand powerless to get him back. My empty arms mourn the loss and I don't know how to live without him. Was my passion taken when he was stolen from me? And, if I don't get it back, what happens next?

FAITH INTERRUPTED

My faith is gone, but not dead.
Have I failed, or has my faith failed me?

Why does it choose to live away from me now?
I do not know.

All I know is that what I had is gone
And I do not know who I am without it.

FAITH INTERRUPTED

Amy's Thoughts:

My faith had been ripped away from me and I didn't know how to act. Everything I knew to be true had changed. I did feel like it had been stolen from me. I felt sick to my stomach most days and fought to keep from breaking down. I remember the struggle it was just to go to the grocery store each week. I would wear my sunglasses inside to hide the tears that would fall down my cheek as I moved food from the shelf to my cart. I was mourning a loss I did not even understand.

I could not have explained to you why I felt bad or even given words to those feelings. But sometimes I could write and the words would paint a picture of my pain. When I read them now—years later—I remember the emotions inside me as I wrote. The pain flairs up again. But now I have the perspective of time and healing. Now I better understand the loss I was feeling.

I felt such confusion and heartbreak in this season of my life. I felt abandoned by God and also abandoned by my own inner faith. The emptiness and loss was part of me for a long time.

I thought it was all I was left with.

Dr. Dave's Counsel:

My sister is seven years younger than me. Though there were times she was a thorn in my side, I always thought of her as my own little princess. Well, to be honest, there were a few times that I thought of her as an opposing running-back to be tackled when we played football in the den...but that's a story for another time.

I remember times when my parents would discipline my sister for something she had done. I would hear those cries of pain coming from her in the discipline, and anger would rise like a flash flood within me. Whatever was happening, it needed to stop. That was 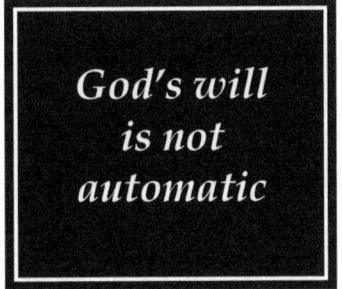 my perspective...that was my world. Of course, there was nothing I could do. But I remember those feelings like it was yesterday.

As I reflect, I realize the anger came from a lack of understanding of what was going on. My parents had a perspective that I did not. There was a behavior in my sister that they wanted to remove from her, not for their benefit, but for hers. I get that now.

FAITH INTERRUPTED

What's Really Going On? is a vivid portrayal of what it feels like to not understand what is happening around you. And by that I mean to SIGNIFICANTLY not understand what is happening!

In Christian pop psychology, I frequently read well-written pieces from well-meaning people who hit the cliché button. All things work together for good...blessed are those that mourn...nothing can separate us....You know what I mean. These are great scriptures, but sometimes it's timing that's key. The words aren't helping me understand, so they really aren't helping. What I need is a revelation from God.

Jeremiah 33:3 gives us the promise that we need in these moments:

> *"Call to me, and I will answer."*

There is more to the verse, I know. But the core of what we need is there. When I call, He will answer.

Perfect.

So what's really going on right now?

About 8 years after the greatest trial of my 50 years on earth, God finally gave me the answer that I had been seeking as to why. It was a beautiful moment when He revealed it. So much healing had taken place, so much

FAITH INTERRUPTED

time had passed. I was at the place I could receive it, and understand it. God simply said...

"Not everything that I want to happen, happens."

So much Scripture now came into clear focus for me. Times that God expressed His will, and people disobeyed what He wanted. People go to hell every day, and God doesn't want that to happen to any of them.

This can be a frustrating realization, but it was a great one for me. God's will is not automatic, so bad things happen to good people. God didn't and doesn't cause people to do evil things. He just doesn't stop them by violating their will. Sometimes there are miraculous interventions in a good way, but just watch the news and you can see that frequently there are not. When God showed me what was really going on in my situation years before, I realized what had really happened, why it had really happened, and how my actions were really ok in the situation. It didn't change the wreckage, but it did change my heart – and my relationship with God.

So ask Him, *"What's really going on?"* and wait for what could be a surprising answer.

FAITH INTERRUPTED

8
Canyon's Edge

Journal Excerpt:

I walk along the canyon's edge, unsure of how I got here or how to move to safer ground.

To my left, a wall of smooth, grey rock that rises one hundred feet above my outstretched trembling hands. Without crevices or caves, it offers little comfort and no protection for my weary body. To the right the rocky path falls away, sometimes crumbling beneath my very feet. The loose rocks fall and bounce against the boulders below, crashing over and over again until finally they crumble into pieces and land in the cold, clear river below. The river looks peaceful and steady as it flows—the final resting place of all who challenge the mountain's edge.

The path is hard and cruel, but I cannot turn back.

There is nothing behind me, so I am forced to press on, through the days of exhausting heat that would take away my will to go on; through the cold, cold nights where rest would surely bring death. Through the pounding rains and the biting winds I continue to walk.

I walk because I cannot run.
I walk because there is nothing else to do...

The worst moments—the most terrifying that seem to take the breath right out of my lungs-- are when I tumble and fall. Time stands still as I struggle to gain control and find footing. I slip over the edge, grasping for something to hold onto, screaming in terror as everything I reach

FAITH INTERRUPTED

for gives way and crumbles in my grasp.

For a moment I am suspended on the edge of this rock looking at the jagged earth beneath as a tragic grave. Then in a moment of sheer will and determination I pull myself to safety. My body collapses against the rock, chest heaving, eyes wide with fear, body shaking. Survival comes at a high price, draining me of all my strength.

Once again, I walk along the canyon's edge.
I cannot go back, so I move forward
...unsure of how I got here
...unsure of where the path will lead.

Amy's Thoughts:

After our disaster, I was frozen in fear at different times. We had lost jobs and the means to support our family. I'd lost my emotional strength and felt I would disconnect in a dangerous way. When I wrote this, all I could see is what would happen if I fell off that cliff. I couldn't see anything to hold on to in order to pull myself to safety. That is a very scary place to be in life: to be afraid to hold on AND afraid to let go at the same time. Everything became about survival and all the smaller issues of life just disappeared.

One of my earliest part-time jobs seemed as tenuous as that cliff. I had found a pretty safe place to work and was beginning to enjoy it just a little…maybe even feel a little bit of stability coming back into my world. I had some success and began to build a relationship with a woman in the office. But, I was weak emotionally. I cried sometimes as I began to open up to her. And then one day I had a panic attack. I started to hyperventilate. Tears were uncontrollable. I felt sick to my stomach and my heart was racing. A panic attack itself is its own problem, but on top of that I was embarrassed and afraid of the consequences of this to my new job. That made the panic even worse! There was no stopping a full-on attack. I had to leave to regain my emotions and recover from the physical consequences of the attack.

FAITH INTERRUPTED

Psalm 40 1-2 says,

> "I waited patiently for the Lord; he turned to me and heard my cry. He lifted me out of the slimy pit, out of the mud and mire; he set my feet on a rock and gave me a firm place to stand."

What I did not know until later was that my manager was very familiar with the symptoms of panic attacks. She understood. It was ok. I wouldn't be fired. In fact, it just served to build a deeper friendship of understanding and support. Now, as I look back, I can see how my feet were placed on a firm rock in the midst of the "mud and mire" of my condition.

In the moment, I was too overwhelmed by my surroundings to realize that God had heard my cry and had me in a safe place. I was so afraid. But now I can see that I was on solid ground. And that safe place gave me time to heal a little and begin to walk again. God was there lifting me up and placing me on a rock even when I couldn't comprehend it.

Dr. Dave's Counsel:

You've heard it said that "perception is reality." That is actually not technically true – perception is really just perception. But **to our emotions**, what we perceive is the truth that we live in. When Amy wrote this journal entry, she was on the path to recovery. Things were getting better. Life was getting back to normal. Then, seemingly without notice, fear would overwhelm her. It would obliterate her perspective. It would take over her thoughts and emotions. It was REAL. It was TRUE. And it was all encompassing. Anyone who has ever truly been in the grip of fear knows this feeling intimately.

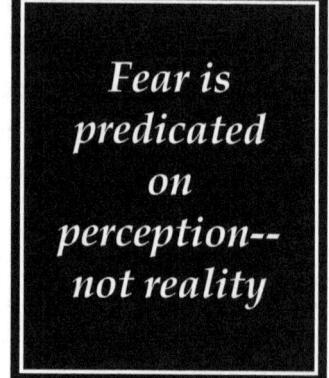

Fear is predicated on perception-- not reality

What she eventually discovered was that the fear was predicated on a perception of the situation, not the reality of the situation. In fact, God had placed her in a very safe place, in the life of a very safe woman, who also intimately knew the pain Amy was experiencing. This was a person who would support her, encourage her, and ultimately be a living example that the fear was actually surmountable.

FAITH INTERRUPTED

This is the key point...**Amy did not perceive that God was doing good things around her, but He was.** She couldn't see it. She couldn't feel it. She didn't recognize it. But He was.

Remember the story of Elijah's servant (2 Kings 6)? They were camped out on a mountainside awaiting an impending battle. The servant saw the hillside and realized there was a countless army amassed against them and he freaked out in fear. Elijah, a supernatural man of God, and a smart one, realized the servant needed a new perspective. He prayed a simple pray and - BAM! The servant's eyes were opened. This is the passage from which the awesome phrase "chariots of fire" comes from. You see, the servant didn't realize that God was working, but He was. Go back and read 2 Kings 6: 8-17 and see if it helps.

This is the dilemma of an interrupted faith...we use to believe God was working. Then we didn't see Him working anymore, or we see Him NOT working (there is a difference, but it has the same effect) and so our perspective becomes locked in - without God.

Two quick points: (1) the perspective to us is real. The perception is the reality. We can't see Him, and we can't see Him working. Point blank. Period. I'm not in any way invalidating your assertion that God isn't there or isn't working. I'm not challenging you that way.

Embrace the 'godlessness' of your moment if that is where you are. Shout it out to Him. Let Him feel it, all of it. Let Him experience it, just like you are experiencing it.

(2) But ... that doesn't mean He isn't really working. He may, in point of fact, be doing a TON around you that you can't see. He's fine with that. He's fine to be in the shadows. He's fine to operate in our behalf when we are mad at Him. He's fine be our good, good, Father, when we believe He is evil. Normally, we eventually see that His goodness was working. And He is entirely gracious to us when we do.

Perception is reality...

Except when it's not.

PART 2:
THE STRUGGLE

FAITH INTERRUPTED

9
Some Kind of Faith

Journal Excerpt:

I look at familiar words on these precious, worn pages that once brought me comfort and peace.

There is a distance now.

Like someone else's friend.

The words are meaningless to me. The stories are about other people now. The challenges already spent in this life.

My own story seems to be over. I cannot connect with the character I was just one page before.

The setting has changed and the plot seems stagnant. We are on to book two...so, why do the fears of book one still haunt me?

I look up to see the presence of the One who created and holds our world.
I look out to see the end of time overtaken by Him.
But in the middle--in my now--I cannot see Him.
I do not grasp Him.

I believe His presence is real, but I'm still unable to sense it in any way. I guess it is some kind of faith to find that I still believe in the midst of this emptiness.

But trauma has shut down my faith. Not in death but in sleep it lies unconscious.

In some ways I feel the same person is still inside me. I am the same self with my family. But the

FAITH INTERRUPTED

dialog is gone between God and me. The voices that were constant companions for years--questioning, laughing, discussing, dreaming, instructing--are now deafeningly silent.

Is it faith to believe that the voices will resume their conversation one day?

Is it some kind of faith just to believe?

Amy's Thoughts:

I know the theological answer to my desperate question is yes. Yes, it is faith when you believe without believing--when you hope against hope. Dave and I once wrote a song with the line: *"faith is knowing what you just can't know."*

Psalms 34:18 says:

> *"The Lord is close to the brokenhearted and saves those who are crushed in spirit."*

I didn't know it then, but I was brokenhearted. And the Lord was close by. Looking back now, I see that He was a gentle, quiet presence in my life as I healed. And it was *some kind of faith* that kept me going. I see now that it was the most genuine of all faiths because it was a knowing in my gut even though I just couldn't know or perceive it at the time…that God is good.

That is some kind of faith.

Dr. Dave's Counsel:

Faith is faith.

This is a simple, yet incomprehensible truth. To believe, no matter how much or how little, is faith. There is much talk in the Christian world about grandiose faith: faith that moves mountains, faith that overcomes, healing faith, and breakthrough faith. The list goes on and on. At times, Christian leaders seek to explain why God does not appear to be functioning "correctly" (according to their theological box) by placing the blame on a lack of faith. I agree that a lack of faith can impact our reality.

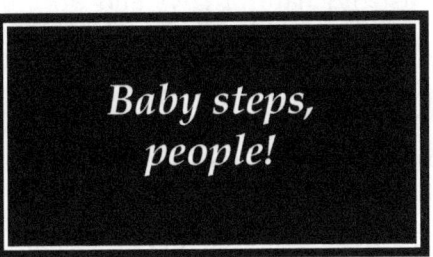

BUT...

It is just too easy to blame faith. This is a simple statement: *"without faith it is impossible to please God"* (Heb. 11:6). How much is required? There is no answer given. Here is what is stated:

> *"Anyone who comes to him must believe that he exists and that he rewards those who earnestly seek him."*

FAITH INTERRUPTED

The mere desire to have faith in the midst of a storm, however small that amount of faith might be, reveals the fact that we believe He IS, and that He answers. Remember this, according to Jesus a mustard seed amount of faith can move a mountain into the ocean (Matt 17:20). A mustard seed ...

That's *some kind of faith,* isn't it?

There have been times in my life when I have seen God suspend natural laws and do miracles in my presence. In some of those cases extreme faith was in operation, in others, God just did what God does. It seems to me that the key to it all isn't the amount of faith; it is the God on the other end of it.

What Amy and I learned through our season of disconnect is that there was still a shred of faith within us. There was still a morsel. There was still a thread that connected us.

That's *some kind of faith* isn't it?

As you journey back from the deep, remember, it's not the amount of faith that impresses God... **it's the existence of faith that pleases him.**

Baby steps, people.
God delights in baby steps!

10
Life Comes at You Sideways

Journal Excerpt:

Suddenly, without warning, our world shifts. And with the shift, our life is off balance. This is not what we expected, not even what we had dreamed. It feels more like a nightmare!

At first we cannot breathe. We stagger and gasp for air as the world begins to blacken around us. We hold on to one thought that will keep us from going down. Voices are blurred and we pray to God for help.

Next comes an awful silence.

FAITH INTERRUPTED

It may last for, hours, days, or months.

I'm not dreaming, this is my new reality. Nothing can change it. The mind then races toward an escape. Running, searching, grasping at...nothing!

Where can I go?
What can I do?
There has to be a way out!

Eventually, the mind entertains the Spirit...
And hope is escorted in!

Hope because the Creator is present.
Hope because we will stand again...

Amy's Thoughts:

Psalm 23 says the *"Lord is my shepherd...He leads me beside quiet waters, he restores my soul."* But it also says that *"I walk through the valley of the shadow of death"* surrounded by evil!

Life is always twisting and turning in ways I could never have anticipated. It seems that when we are at peace we are looking for adventure and when we are in turmoil we are begging for peace. When will we learn to expect change to come?

In the movie, *Serenity* (one of our family favorites!), Shepherd Book says of the enemy, *"they'll come at you sideways..."* Well, LIFE comes at us sideways, doesn't it? At least that has been my experience. Sometimes evil comes, but sometimes it is just change and life. Sometimes it is a series of unfortunate events that just doesn't seem to stop. Life is unpredictable.

When I wrote those words in my journal...

I didn't know.

I didn't know the changes would be the best thing that could have happened for my son, Josh. I didn't know his dreams would become larger than Texas and he would reach for things he never thought possible before.

I didn't know that my daughter, Chelsea, would emerge strong, rather than broken, from the trauma. That she would become the amazing, intellectual and spiritual leader that she has become!

I didn't know my husband and I would find our biggest adventures ever and help people in ways we had never dreamed.

I didn't know that it would begin to make sense…that I would see God's hand and…above all His compassion and love for us.

I didn't know.

And I don't know the answers today. I can't tell you where God will take Dave and me. But, now I begin to see where He is heading.

…It's the next step, of course!

Dr. Dave's Counsel:

There comes a point when we turn the corner, or at least we catch our first glimpse around the corner. *Turning the corner* is different from *a change of trajectory* that we have discussed before. Here, the visceral pain has come to an end. There has been a season without trauma. A time without the emotions dialed all the way up to ten. A time when things begin to have a rhythm again, a rhythm that doesn't revolve around "crazy." The world is entirely different from what it was pre-trauma, but it is settling down--at least a little bit--from the tumult.

It is in this moment we must pause and consider our recovery. It is our very first time to consider who we want to be IN LIGHT of what is happened. There are really only three options, and the decision we make now will determine much of our future.

- Will we be forever defined by the trauma, diminished from the person we once were?
- Will we be forever afraid that it will happen again, and thus live in a newfound fearful state?
- Or will it be a point of transition for us as we embark on a new journey, perhaps one that we never anticipated?

In the enthusiasm of my youth, I believe I would have

added a fourth option that went something like this: "or will I be the overcomer who is undeterred, and courageously carries forth?" That is the ideal, of course, but it is unrealistic. The death of a spouse, or a dream, or a relationship…whatever it is that dies, will certainly leave a mark. And that is as it should be. We aren't a bulletproof Marvel superhero. We are human, flesh-and-blood people who live in a dangerous world filled with sharp objects. It's inevitable that our heart will get cut at some point. Sometimes, that cut will be deep, and could be emotionally and spiritually life-threatening.

> *Consider WHO you want to be in light of what has happened*

Let's think of Jesus. Even He was marked by death. And it's a good thing that He was. Remember doubting Thomas? He wasn't so much a doubter, as he was one who wanted to live in the real, rather than in fantasy. In John 20:24-29 we have this amazing passage where he demands to see the marks of death in Jesus body or he will not believe. Jesus then comes to him and says…

> "Put your finger here; see my hands.
> Reach out your hand and put it into my side.
> Stop doubting and believe."

FAITH INTERRUPTED

Jesus wasn't defined by the death. He wasn't still dead. He rose from the dead, all the while carrying the marks of that death.

Who will you be **after** this trauma? What will be your personality? How will you relate to others? What will be your baseline emotional state? All of these are within your power to determine, and it is best to start that process once you can see around the corner.

FAITH INTERRUPTED

11
Raw God

Journal Excerpt:

There is a rugged wildness to the woods—a growing, spreading, uncontrollable wildness that we <u>try</u> to tame. We mow the grass in neat, geometric lines. We cut down trees and we trim weeds by the bank of the creek. But the wildness returns every time, like an unwelcome house guest. Given enough time, paths will become overgrown, the creek will disappear from human view, and the dense woods will be impassable once again.

I try to tame God the same way we tame our yards.

I want to take all He is and make Him into a beautifully manicured idea that works for me.

Theology books do that
Respected philosophies do that
Mainstream religions do that
Our churches do that
I do that.

But God is wild and untamable.
He is raw.

And His greatest beauty is found where man has not touched anything.

FAITH INTERRUPTED

Amy's Thoughts:

I have been slow to learn this lesson. I thought if I lived right, the results were inevitable. A leads to B, B leads to C, and so on. But that is not true. Not even most of the time is it true! Over and over and OVER again God has up-ended my life, moved me to a different home, different job, different church, different life. All of my plans have been changed, every time.

God is God and He will do what He wants.

He is not to be controlled by us. C.S. Lewis in his book, *The Chronicles of Narnia*, says of the lion, **"He is not tame, but He is good."** The lion is a picture of God in the book and...God is not tame. The word "tame" makes me think of an animal that behaves the way his master has trained him. But, who could control God? Certainly not His creation! I cannot tell God what to do...cannot persuade Him by my good works or my good words. He is God. He is wild and untamed.

We can recognize that in raw nature — and raw God — is the greatest beauty of all.

I want to know this RAW God.

Not a God I make up in my mind, but the real thing!

FAITH INTERRUPTED

And this God—the real one—is unfathomable. His power is immense. His reach is beyond what I can even comprehend. That feels dangerous and unsetting. But I want to know the REAL God and have a relationship with Him!

I need to recognize that He is God…but I can trust that He is always good. I can trust Him with me and those I love. He won't take my life where I expect, but He loves me and He is good to me always. And this is the new faith emerging for me. This new faith understands from experience that God is larger than I can ever fathom.

Some of the worst moments of my life have been the best of God's goodness to me. At the time, of course, I did not see that. For years I did not see that. But now, with new perspective, I can see what God was doing and know it was His grace and love that turned my life upside down so He could fix it. Because God sees from eternity and knows all, His understanding is beyond us. We cannot control Him, or anticipate His actions. I will spend my lifetime trying to better understand Him and know Him. But, above all, I believe that I can trust Him. I do trust Him.

He is not tame, but He is good.

FAITH INTERRUPTED

Dr. Dave's Counsel:

As humans, we are prone to define things from our own perspective. It brings us comfort. It brings us security. I know I do that. Or at least I did. I can't really guess how many times I have heard Jeremiah 29:11…

For I know the plans I have for you, declares the LORD, plans to prosper you and not to harm you, plans to give you hope and a future.

> **God is a wrecking ball!**

Our natural inclination is to interpret that verse this way, "*God sees my life, He wants good things for me, He will not harm me, so only good things are coming to me.*" In fact this very teaching is at the core of some modern theological movements. If we believe a certain way, and speak about it that way, it will happen. That never involves calamity, and if it does, there is fault somewhere other than God.

Poppycock.

FAITH INTERRUPTED

God is a wrecking ball! It's a part of His nature. When our lives need to be adjusted, God is the "Great Adjuster." (Insert Jesus in the Temple wreaking havoc, here). He can tune us up in ways that we could never have imagined. While I completely agree with the band, HouseFires, which sings He is a *Good, Good, Father,* sometimes good dads bring pain in order to bring growth, or safety. I remember my dad once hurt my arm as he grabbed me to pull me out of the path of an oncoming car. That's good pain.

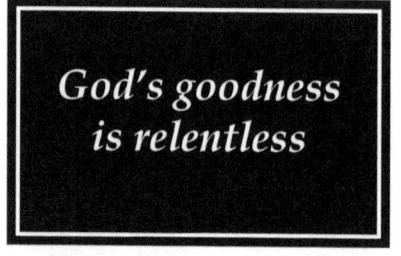

It's a matter of perspective. Job got this when he said (2:10)...

"Shall we accept good from God, and not trouble?"

It is absolutely true that He is ALWAYS and ONLY doing good, but our perspective of good can be way off. We think of good as pain-free, stable, and safe. Sometimes pain is good (childbirth). Sometimes security is painful (eternal security is predicated on it – aka the Cross). Quite frequently when we are years removed from an event, we look back and realize the peaceful, painless and safe JAIL we were a prisoner in before the cataclysmic event that God used to free us. Today, we can't see that. I'm not saying this to diminish your pain.

FAITH INTERRUPTED

I don't want to diminish your pain. Embrace it, and as I have said a number of times, YELL it to GOD. He's a big boy, he can take it! In fact He WANTS it. But we must remember that God's goodness is relentless. Like the lush grass that grows in Amy's opening journal writing, we may want to freeze the picture of our yard once it is cut. But we can't. It just keeps growing.

God's Goodness will never stop.

Never...Ever.

FAITH INTERRUPTED

12
The Stuff of Me

Journal Excerpt:

I prayed and worked,
sacrificed, gave, counseled, taught,
wrote, sang, listened,
loved, cheered, wept
...all to know Him more.
All to be what He wanted me to be.

And so, when my life crashed like a car spun into oncoming traffic, I found myself unable to continue...unable to even speak to God.

I am surprised to find that my essence—the stuff of me—remains the same.

I am ME without the props.
I am ME without an audience.
I am ME.

And He is not changed by the death around me.
He is not dependent on my devotion or my understanding.
We, God and I, are not changed.

No one or nothing has taken that away.
Although my life has been stripped from me,
although I am broken in spirit,
although I cannot turn to look for God...we are one together and that has not changed.

So I will—when I can—go on from here.

And I will carry with me the stuff of who I am.

FAITH INTERRUPTED

Amy's Thoughts:

When my world crashed, I found myself in new surroundings. Most of what had once been a part of my life changed. The moorings or ropes that held me to my life were ripped away.

We all have these ropes. Mine were my nights with girlfriends, helping the kids with schoolwork, buying groceries, my counseling and writing, the church where I prayed and served. It was where we ate lunch and enjoyed weekend motorcycle rides. It was the house full of our closest friends and quiet walks with my husband. A thousand little things make up the individual lives that we are living. These things hold us and become a part of what makes us whole. But in a moment, my ropes were gone. They were lost.

It was months later that I began to realize that the inner presence was still there. My dialogue with God had ceased, but He was still there. And I realized that my true self with my ideals and values were the same. I related to those I love the same way I always had. I began to feel like myself again.

I was still ME inside, even though everything around me was different. God's Spirit still lived in me. My true essence is entwined with the heart of God through the

Spirit of God. We are one. And THAT was still there. I found great comfort in this realization. It was like finding one of my ropes to hold onto again. I wasn't completely adrift anymore...and had never actually been without Him.

Dr. Dave's Counsel:

This chapter is the core of this book. When we were working through the title, we weren't sure whether it should be *Faith Interrupted* or *Faith Interrupted?* That little question mark was the tip of the spear. Retrospectively, was our faith really interrupted? Is that what really happened? In this chapter I'm just going to share my heart, rather than explain or encourage. There is SO MUCH to this: so much Bible, so much psychology. But sometimes it's better to just hear someone's *heart*. That is what is happening here. Enjoy.

Here is my deepest lesson from this almost 10-year season. **Faith is a partnership**. Faith is a two-way street. Faith is God AND me working together for this relationship and this life. It's not just me reaching to Him, believing even when I don't.

Sometimes things are easy. It's all fine, things are going well. All is peaceful. Whatever challenges there are, they are outside of me, not within. I look over my world and I say with God in Genesis 1, *it is good*. In these situations it feels as if I've got this. I'm in a great place. My faith is strong and it's operating like a well-oiled machine.

FAITH INTERRUPTED

When there are trying circumstances, my faith (which is a gift from Him) is strong. This is how I basically lived, right up to the moment of disaster. Honestly, I can only remember the occasional time when what I faced approached the limit of my faith. I've seen miracles; I have had them occur from my hands and words. But I had never before reached the end of my faith. I had never even seen it afar off.

When disaster hit, I blew past the end of my faith at a million miles an hour. I was launched into this abyss of unfamiliarity and darkness like nothing I had ever known.

My faith locked up.
It stopped working.

It didn't respond. It just disappeared. The TRUTH of it was there. I didn't doubt the WORD. I just couldn't respond. At all. I just navigated the disaster to the best of my ability with my faith on hiatus.

So here was the lesson. **He just took it--all of it**. He made up for it. He didn't just make up the difference…I was actually operating at 0% for a while. So He operated at 100%. I know that now a decade later. He didn't vanish. He didn't get frustrated. He didn't feel neglected. He didn't pull back. Our journey and relationship was ALL HIM.

Ironically, this is absolutely theologically sound. Our salvation is entirely Him. All we do is say "yes" and receive Him. He took our place. It is *"not by works, so that no one can boast "*(Ephesians 2:8-9). My faith is exactly the same in its operation. It's all Him, not me. That does NOT mean that I have no part in it, but it means that when I CANNOT have a part in it, He does it. I never knew that. I guess I should say I never FELT that.

I feel it now. I KNOW it. In the deepest place where my knower is, I know it. God's got me. Whatever may come. He's not going to be disappointed and walk away. He's just going to be there for me.

It's a partnership.

And He is the greatest partner ever.

FAITH INTERRUPTED

13
Disconnected

Journal Excerpt:

I jammed it all roughly into an old cardboard box. I carried it to the basement, pushed it into the corner and covered it up with an old wool blanket, hoping to never see it again.

That SHOULD have worked.
I thought it would work.
It even SEEMED to work at first.

But the box was always there, lurking in the edge of my mind. I could hear the scary music playing each time I walked past the stairs...like the music score from a horror flick!

Finally, it was time to face my memories, despite the pain.

I made myself go down there and open the old cardboard box. Sitting there on the floor, I pulled everything out and spread it onto the cold cement.

As everything lay scattered around me...
I realized that I had been living without a part of me.

I missed me.
And, I wanted some of me back.

I did not want to put it in the box in the corner again. Yes, this last season of my life had ended very badly. I may have scars for years. Some of it has been good; some of it tragically life-altering.

FAITH INTERRUPTED

All of it has been me!
I don't want to lose a precious part of myself because I was hiding from the pain.

I've got all of my stuff with me again with no more scary music playing in the background!

Time to walk back upstairs...

Amy's Thoughts:

Life quite often throws us surprises we did not wish for and certainly would not have asked for. When those circumstances are particularly unpleasant, we try to disconnect them from who we are. And so, we become **fragmented.** But, when we can connect the pieces and see our life as a linear journey, our heart can settle down, and our ability to look forward is renewed.

My job search was a great illustration of this. I found it very difficult to present my life on a resume that would make sense to an employer. I was stuck for a while figuring out how it all flowed together. I felt as green as a college graduate hunting for that first job. My years before moving to Texas seemed like a different life. It was disconnected from where I was at the time. Once I began to figure out a career direction, I was able to frame my past experience in a way that made sense. I was able to use my past accomplishments to get the next job, and then use those skills IN the next job.

And once I had a new direction in my life as a whole, I slowly was able to reach back into my past and draw the good out and use it. I can now access all that was good before my life radically changed. Our whole family can now look at our lives from a new perspective. The kids look back on their childhoods with fond memories and

FAITH INTERRUPTED

the move to Texas as a life-changing event that brought them to the great place they are now. My husband and I now reach down to the foundations we laid years ago and look for new ways to help people through life's struggles.

I feel whole now. Even the painful times are part of who I am. Now that I have moved away from them, I can use them to be a better person, and even share them with you in this book.

Dr. Dave's Counsel:

What Amy speaks about here in *Disconnected* is the psychological coping mechanism called compartmentalization. In an effort to assist us with surviving an emotional trauma in our lives, our minds can create a barrier between our consciousness and the event(s). This takes place in varying degrees with individuals based upon their internal resources and the depth of the pain. But the purpose is the same…functionality.

> *Even the painful times are part of who I am*

We may be more familiar with this concept in our day-to-day world than we realize. I was recently talking with a man who was contemplating the sale of a business. His wife was the primary person who had started it, and worked in it for nearly 5 years. As he and I were discussing the situation he said, "She wanted me to come to talk to you about the potential sale because she thought she would get emotional about it. To me it's just business, but to her it is personal." Exactly. This is a form of compartmentalization. There are scientific reasons why men seem more able to do this than women, most of which have to do with complexity (women) verses simplicity (men), but the reality of the

FAITH INTERRUPTED

truth is similar. Every single one of us has the ability to compartmentalize.

Spiritually speaking, and emotionally as well, compartmentalization is at best only a short-term fix. It allows us to function in the moment, but merely postpones the inevitable where we must deal directly with what took place. We can't bury the trauma, because it just won't go away. It never will. Eventually we must come to terms with what happened and begin to see our new selves in light of it. When our faith is able to re-ignite again, our first task is frequently to begin to understand who we are in light of what happened, and who we will be from this point forward in light of it.

Our pastor early in our recovery in Texas (Pastor Kerry Shook, Woodlands Church, Woodlands, TX) used to frequently preach about God's great power by saying we are *"turning our mess...into a message!"*

This is absolutely true. There comes a time in our lives when the compartmentalization is no longer needed because we are not trapped in the avoidance of pain. We can see what happened, recognize its place in our lives, understand what our future may hold, and reengage in our journey again. The starting point may be different, and the earthly direction may have changed, but the ultimate destination is fixed--knowing and pleasing Him once again.

14
When Vanity Makes Sense

Journal Excerpt:

I never liked the man and disagreed with everything he taught. His research was solid, his facts were right. But his conclusions were wrong every time—all wrong.

How could he say life was without meaning? My life had such purpose. Why did he conclude that no one can make a difference when I clearly was changing my world?

Solomon said it doesn't matter who you are or what you do, life is going to take you down and destroy you. You can't stop it or even explain it.

It will happen.

But I kept fighting—for years struggling against that force. "I get up and go on. It makes me stronger. I must overcome!" He said that good comes to both the just and the unjust. I saw that. But I worked to find more good in my world.

Finally, I entered into the worst fight of my life. I was struck down and there was no getting up after that.

Once again, I read his words. This time I understood. "Vanity, vanity...it is all vanity." All I have done in this life for good seemed to vanish on the wind. All my efforts were stolen by my enemy. He is a wicked thief who has left me nothing but ashes of wasted life.

"Both destruction and good come to every man—good or bad." And I see that the truth has

given birth in me. If there is eternity in anything I have done for good, it has already taken flight. What comes next does not matter.
It will be good, or it will be evil.

Vanity, vanity. It is all vanity.

FAITH INTERRUPTED

Amy's Thoughts:

I grew up with a happy childhood (thank you, mom and dad!) and a romantic view of life. I was convinced that good things happened to good people...bad things happened to bad people. That the world was just in the end and everything would work its way around to being right. But, that just isn't true. When we approach life with the wrong facts, it's hard to get past the feelings of betrayal when things go wrong.

I had been betrayed.

Bad things do happen to good people. Life is unpredictable. Life can be cut short. This is the way the world works. Solomon was reflecting on his observations of life and they were correct. In Ecclesiastes 9:1ff he concludes that everyone (good and evil) is in God's hands and no one knows their own fate. When life knocked me down, I did come to believe his words were true.

However, in my disillusioned state, I missed the most important words that Solomon spoke. In verses 7-10 he tells us how to live in light of these facts:

"Go, eat your food with gladness, and drink your wine with a

FAITH INTERRUPTED

joyful heart, for God has already approved what you do. Always be clothed in white, and always anoint your head with oil. Enjoy life with your wife, whom you love, all the days of this meaningless life that God has given you under the sun – all your meaningless days. For this is your lot in life and in your toilsome labor under the sun. Whatever your hand finds to do, do it with all your might, for in the realm of the dead, where you are going, there is neither working nor planning nor knowledge nor wisdom."

In the midst of this unpredictable life, here is what Solomon recommends: first, he says to enjoy life and its gifts as long as you have them. Be thankful and embrace what you have. Enjoy prosperity and wealth when you have it; enjoy simple pleasures when money fails you. Treasure your loved ones, honor them, do good things for them and with them while you have the chance. Make a difference in their lives. Embrace the beauty and mystery of the stuff of life around you. Enjoy the sunset, play in the ocean,...and eat chocolate!

Second, always be in a state of celebration. Dress up and get out there! There are enough reasons life gives us to be held down and pushed back. Let's celebrate the victories and successes. Remember to look back just long enough to see how far you've come!

In those early years in Texas, our family found ways to have fun together and we celebrated each victory together, no matter how small. That first year, we celebrated moving to Texas. We focused on every good thing that had happened since we moved--that first job, and the second, the kids' school accomplishments, finding a friend, getting health insurance, moving into our own apartment. Now every August we celebrate moving to Texas as a family tradition. What was initially a terrible crisis, and our own personal Alamo, has given way to the victory at San Jacinto!

> *Look back just long enough to see how far you've come!*

Third, enjoy your marriage and your spouse (and I would add your family). Several years ago we lost a great deal. But we still were a close family. We supported each other, loved each other, fought for each other. That made all the difference in each of us finding our way to a new life and finding hope and happiness.

Fourth, Solomon said to work hard while you are able to work. God made us with this need to be productive and work. Use your work to make a difference in people's lives by what you do and say. Life is unpredictable and brief, so embrace it, jump into it, take risks and search out new challenges.

FAITH INTERRUPTED

Our family has a way to remind ourselves that life is hard and we just need to push through. Whenever someone faces a great disappointment or unexpected disaster we say, *"This will make a great story one day!"*

And we go on.

Life isn't easy. It's actually quite difficult at times. But we need to follow Solomon's advice: enjoy the blessings when you have them, always celebrate, enjoy your family, and work hard while you can.

Live a great story!

Dr. Dave's Counsel:

Amy's words here give us a glimpse into our pre and post trauma thinking. Before trauma we are idealistic. After trauma we are pessimistic. Solomon encourages us to be realistic. It is all about how we are processing the information at hand. As a counselor for more than 20 years, I have helped my share of traumatized people. What I have found is that by-and-large the gaze of these individuals becomes fixed, and generally it is fixed on the trauma. They are focused on what they had, then they shift their focus to what they have now, and their mind does the math. And this is the formula that their mind naturally uses:

THEN – NOW = LOSS

They had more before the trauma and then focus much of their attention on the loss. It just looms larger and larger, something like this ...

LOSS

LOSS

LOSS

FAITH INTERRUPTED

That probably rings a bell for you. Part of survivorship is understanding that mental process, and moving into a new pattern of thinking. What Solomon encourages us to do is to **live in the moment**. Recall the words from the passage ...

> *"Go, eat your food with gladness, and drink your wine with a joyful heart, for God has already approved what you do. Always be clothed in white, and always anoint your head with oil. Enjoy life...whatever your hand finds to do, do it with all your might!"*

You can hear the focus on living in the present, without the glare of the past, or in consideration of the future. There definitely comes a point in your recovery where this is doable. And that is the moment that you apply the truth. If you find yourself reading this and your innards are exploding with "you don't understand!" and "how could I forget?", or something along those lines, it just isn't time yet. Eventually you will be there, and when you are you will assist your recovery by doing this simple exercise.

Jesus said, don't worry about tomorrow, because tomorrow has enough worries of its own (Matthew 6:34). It's almost as if He is channeling Solomon. Our task is to find the things that are happening around us right now that are positive things, and acknowledge those: a sunrise or sunset, the beauty of lightning or a summer shower, a butterfly, breath, delicious food, whatever. You can find it. Within you is a person who used to find those things. He or she is still there. So when you are ready…Live in the moment.

PART 3:
THE SURVIVING

FAITH INTERRUPTED

15
Moment of Surprise!

Journal Excerpt:

I felt it last night. An old melody was sung, gentle words of God and life were spoken...and it didn't sting. For the first time in years the wound did not smart as life brushed up against it.

I was slashed with a jagged-edged knife back then. The pain was excruciating. Over time I began to function again, but always felt fresh pain when anything got close to the wound. At first, even air seemed to be an assault on me.

Months ago the bleeding stopped and a thick scab formed, making me numb to feeling there.

FAITH INTERRUPTED

Now, the scab has healed, getting thinner and thinner over time...until yesterday, when I realized that it is gone. I touch the skin and there is no searing pain. I rub the scar and flashes of the crime do not rush into my mind and fill me with fear anymore. There is new baby skin where the wound had been. And so, I touch it gently, carefully. There is still some numbness beneath the surface, but the pain is gone.

I couldn't bear to bring this to Him...

I couldn't even force myself to look at it. So, I looked away and tried to find things to distract me. And that worked until something would brush up against me and fresh pain would rush through me again.

Then, somehow...quietly...He came.

He must have stitched my skin together and

stopped the bleeding. And He must have gently rubbed salve on the wound to make it heal so fast. There were times I thought the pain would never end. I thought I would carry this all my life. But--quite suddenly--I realize that I am starting to feel whole again. I didn't see it happen but it did.

When did I begin to breathe without hesitation?
When did I stop limping from the pain?
I don't remember.

Thank God.
Thank you, God.
It doesn't hurt anymore...

FAITH INTERRUPTED

Amy's Thoughts:

Psalms 147:3 says, *"He heals the brokenhearted and binds up their wounds."*

I don't know how He did it and I don't know when. In my stillness, I was waiting for him to bind up my wounds and heal what was broken. And He did.

Deep wounds scar us for life—even after the pain has receded. What we live through continues to shape and define who we become. But the rawness will be healed with the gentle hands of our Father.

Psalms 145:4 says that one generation will speak about God's works to the next generation. And I do that today. I share what God has done for me. He healed my wounds and He carried me when I couldn't walk. I didn't realize it at the time. I felt abandoned and alone. I felt quite hopeless. I couldn't even ask God to come. I didn't know that all along He was healing me.

Now I can celebrate His goodness and sing His praises for my children and grandchildren to understand. I share my pain and hurt so that you understand the miracle God performed.

If there is no wound, there is nothing to heal.

FAITH INTERRUPTED

I opened my heart to show you the wound. I showed you my pain and bleeding. I was weak and I was without hope. This is not a story of my own efforts. This is the story of a sincere, flawed person who lost her way when bad things happened. I thought I had lost it all, but I found that I had more than I ever imagined!

FAITH INTERRUPTED

Dr. Dave's Counsel:

When I was growing up we didn't have Powerball, or Mega Millions. We had Publisher's Clearing House. (I know some of you reading don't even know what I'm talking about.) What I loved about those TV spots was the surprise! There's a TV crew creeping up someone's lawn with a six-foot check and their name on it. The doorbell rings and a guy comes to the door in a pair of gym shorts and a ratty shirt, and finds out he's a millionaire. What's interesting to me is that all of that had been in the works for a while...he just didn't know it.

Sometimes our healing is just like that. We're living our lives in survival mode, or trying to just survive in survival mode. It's all pretty laborious. And then in a moment, we wake up and realize that the pain isn't there. It can be jarring at first, like something's missing-- but it's a *good* missing.

In my own journey, much of what I dealt with was financial. We faced relentless bill collecting, without a dime to our name. For months it went on and on. Jobs couldn't quiet the monster. No matter how much we did, or how hard we tried, that beast was never satisfied. I rarely slept through the night. Sometimes the fear was so strong I had to go walk for miles in the middle of the night to exhaust myself to the point that I could catch some sleep. It became a way of life--living under the never-ending pressure of not having enough.

When better jobs came, and money got better, the pressure got better but never really went away. About two years into this thing, I woke up one morning and realized that I had slept through the night. The sun was brighter. The sky was bluer. The trees were greener. It was like I had been wearing dark sunglasses, and now I wasn't. As I look back now I realize that our circumstances didn't really change overnight, my perspective did. And it happened involuntarily.

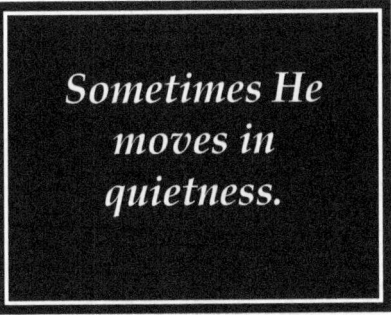
Sometimes He moves in quietness.

Psychologically speaking, this happens when we move from one level of Maslow's Hierarchy to the next. Maslow contended (and I agree) that people have layers of needs. The basic needs must be met (like being safe) before the higher needs can be met (like feeling good about yourself). We don't consciously make the decision to move from one level to the next. It happens where 90% of our intellectual processing takes place, in the sub-conscious. This is why we can wake up one morning and find that things are different...our sub-conscious processed the information and released us. It's

FAITH INTERRUPTED

an awesome experience when it happens.

Spiritually speaking, the laws of nature are subject to the laws of the Spirit. This is the stuff of miracles, when God reaches in and suspends a natural law. An axe might float on water. Time might briefly move backwards. Disease might stop. The dead may live. The jaded may find freedom.

However the freedom comes, whether through subconscious processing or the Spirit of God, it ultimately comes from God. Sometimes He comes crashing into our lives with a miraculous positive change. Sometimes He moves in quietness. But, however it happens, there is that moment of surprise when we realize it is better.

Not perfect. But better.

And the light of hope begins to shine in our hearts again.

16
I Choose to Dance

Journal Excerpt:

If I could, I would run outside every time the violent storm clouds approached, racing to feel the drenching rain beat against my skin. I would stand still like a martyr, waiting for the lightning bolt to strike with its deadly white heat. I long for the crash of thunder to slap my body down and leave me breathless.

Who said I can't dance when life destroys me with deafening thunder and crushing rain? Maybe it lets me know I am alive again if I feel the storm soaking into my clothes, my skin...my soul. The thunder rumbles and shakes the earth beneath me.

And there can be no doubt that I am alive.

So--I choose to dance.

I raise my face to the sky and let the rain slap against me. I glide around and around with determined arms outstretched to embrace the storm. The wind whips my body down like a rag doll in the hands of an angry child. I crumble to the ground as lightning suddenly strikes, blinding my eyes and leaving me staring into white space. I am fully alive when I am in the storm, senses tuned to the powers that rage around me.

I feel excruciating pain—a proof of life—and I am a willing victim in God's hand.

The sun may shine another day.
But right now there is a terrible storm
and I,...I need to dance!

FAITH INTERRUPTED

Amy's Thoughts:

Psalm 77:16-19 says,

"The waters saw you, O God, the waters saw you and writhed; the very depths were convulsed. The clouds poured down water, the skies resounded with thunder; your arrows flashed back and forth. Your thunder was heard in the whirlwind, your lightning lit up the world; the earth trembled and quaked. Your path led through the sea, your way through the mighty waters, though your footprints were not seen."

Storms remind me that I am out of my depth in this life. The thunder that shakes my world like an earthquake, the winds the bear down on me until I am pushed to the ground, the flashes of fire that blind me...these all demonstrate what life has done to me. Along with the blessings and goodness of this life come terrible storms that try to destroy us.

Choosing to dance is embracing the terrible and scary and overwhelming nature of this life while jumping right in the middle of it! Isn't that the way you want to live? Don't you want to experience all of life rather than hide from it? Sometimes I run and hide. This season almost took me out. But *I Choose to Dance* reminds me to reach out and live no matter what the consequences!

FAITH INTERRUPTED

How we choose to approach life and the storms will shape where they lead us. It may take everything inside of you to find the strength to take on the storm. It may try to take everything from you. But how you respond next will define you...the new you...the post trauma you.

I was knocked down and almost out, as you can tell.
I was not strong.
I tried to hide and I was afraid.

But sometimes bravery is found in the very small act of simply standing up. It is getting knocked down again and standing up again. I am not one of those who remained standing. I am not the warrior who fought to the end. I gave up more than once. But I stood back up.
I grabbed my husband's hand and I stood back up.

And then we danced!

Dr. Dave's Counsel:

Psychologically speaking, recovery progression is very much like our human growth cycle. It is born sometime after our trauma (birth). It lives for a season in a very fragile state, requiring assistance to survive (infancy). At some point it begins to move on its own, developing its own direction and identity (childhood). Eventually, it begins to measure itself against others (pubescence), expressing its uniqueness in a variety of circumstances and relationships (adolescence). Ultimately, it settles down into its very own, self-aware, confident expression and then looks to positively impact others (adulthood).

Our new life will be challenged by the old.

What Amy describes is her journey somewhere in the pubescent/adolescent stage. At this point in recovery we are living somewhat normally again. We have discovered a new normal. We have found a new rhythm. And then something happens that reminds us of the past. It could be a phone call, or a smell, or a drive past a certain place. It doesn't matter what it is, but it is a trigger that brings back thoughts of the past. It is in those moments that our new life is challenged by the old. Our childlike recovery is tested to see what it is actually made of. To see how strong it is. And it is in those moments that we can dance.

The childhood instinct is to run. The first time it happens or maybe early in your adolescent recovery, running may be the best course of action. Eventually though, you can stand there, in the moment, and you see what happens.

Eventually, you are able to dance in the storm. Adults can do this. They have an awareness of the power of the storm and the destruction that is possible and they respect it, but they are not paralyzed by it. They know that sometimes things that look really scary are safe after all. Your recovery will face these times. It is ironic that as I write this portion from a hotel room in Austin, Texas, there is a torrential thunderstorm outside. The wind is howling. The thunder is incredible. The sky is lit with lightning strikes. I am not afraid...I am appreciative of its power. This is not a storm to play in, but it's not a storm to be afraid of either. As an adult, I recognize the difference.

I mentioned those involuntary triggers. It could be a graveside. Or it might be a house that you owned and lived in together for many years. It might be where you used to feed your secret life. Whatever, wherever...at some point, you face the storm again.

For Amy and me, that ultimate moment came years after our trauma, when we purposefully journeyed back to the place of our disaster. We were there for a very different, very joyous reason. But we wanted to go back and do a drive-by to test our healing. So we did. For an entire day we drove around to the old familiar places. The roads were the same. Honestly, not much had changed at all. We drove and we talked. We stopped the car and walked. We were in the very place of OUR storm, and what we found was that it lived only in the past as a memory, and not in the present as a hidden threat.

And so we danced!

FAITH INTERRUPTED

17
Child in Heart

Journal Excerpt:

We are the same over time's path
Weather-beaten and worn
Bent and almost buried
But a child in heart

Dreams intact—wishes still lodged deep
We ride the carousel
Our faces to the wind, hanging on!

FAITH INTERRUPTED

Amy's Thoughts:

I honestly feel more like a child than adult most days. It's not so bad to stay connected to that part of me. The simplicity of it all seems to help me face life's challenges. The dreams I had when I was young are still in my heart. What makes me happy, what makes me sing...it is still the same.

Many of us lose touch with that simple, younger self as life wears us down. We push those desires and dreams deep down inside where we can't even find them ourselves. But, then life becomes cold, dry and lifeless.

An excerpt from my book, *I Hope You Eat Chocolate!* says that for many, *"fun and adventure was left on the playground years ago. They feel life has already been decided for them. But, you don't have to stay the victim of what your life has become. You can reach inside – past the boredom and emptiness--to that place where Eternity placed life within...and you can begin to breathe again! Find the magic and the sparkles that were meant to be part of your life! No matter what life has beaten you with or what dangers now lay ahead – the heart of God is part of your soul. It could never be stolen, crushed or killed."*

That child you once were may have had some disappointments and been abused. But, there is still a

FAITH INTERRUPTED

precious heart that can live again—that can dream again. So, let's ride that carousel with our face to the wind!

Dr. Dave's Counsel:

There comes a point in our healing when it is time to re-engage our inner kid, to recall the innocence of youth, and to embrace that again. It's daring, that's for sure, but it is important. You see, until we allow ourselves to become little children again, some portion of us will reside in a damp, dark, dungeon. That doesn't sound very good, does it? Think of it this way--how many of your favorite movies start with the protagonist in a place of darkness, spend the entire movie there, and then end in that same place?

None.

It all starts with belief. We were all wired to be children for our entire lives. Spiritually, we never really grow up on this earth. God will forever be our Father, and we will forever be His children. This is an immutable truth. There will never be a time in my existence that I will cease being a child. I'm guessing you would agree with that. Now, let's apply a phrase from the most popular prayer in Christianity, the Lord's Prayer, and let's go old school with the KJV for Matthew 6:9ff.

> *"Our Father, which art in heaven,*
> *Hollowed be thy name.*

FAITH INTERRUPTED

Thy kingdom come, thy will be done,
On earth, as it is in heaven."

Yep. That just happened. In Heaven I will always be a child. That should be true on earth as well. That should be true for me, even in light of my jaded circumstances.

Listen, what happened to you was real. And it really sucked. And you will forever be changed because of it.

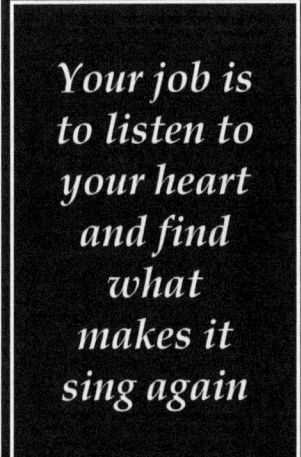

Your job is to listen to your heart and find what makes it sing again

I'm not diminishing that. I'm just saying that there is a world of joy and wonder and discovery BEYOND that. Those circumstances may have tattooed you, but they don't have to DEFINE you, or LIMIT you. And they definitely shouldn't rob you of your kidness. You have to believe that, in order to move forward.

It continues with an embrace. So what are your favorite memories? They may be from your actual, numerical childhood, or they may be from your child-ness, when you felt like a kid. Take a moment and reflect on that, and maybe jot down a list. What was it about those moments that created those feelings? Dig in a little, and investigate that. Ask yourself some questions about it.

FAITH INTERRUPTED

Describe the feelings. Enter in. Remember the details. Allow it to become vivid. Embracing those ACTUAL childish experiences will break off some crustiness from your heart. That's a good thing. It may be a little alarming. You may have fits and starts. That's ok. Go where you can go, then stop when you must. Then come back to it a few days later. If you were paying me to sit on my office couch, we would do this for a season as I guided you back to the familiar of your warm, wonderful, awe-inspiring past. Why? Because this sets up what is next.

It becomes complete with engagement. Now it's time to engage that child-ness again in your life, your new life, as the new person that you are in light of the circumstances, as the person who now refuses to be restrained by your devastation.

Remember this: no one that ever truly loved you would want you to be trapped in the jaded cave. If they loved you, they always wanted the best for you. Being God's son or daughter is the best for you. Explore the things that could bring you joy or wonder. They may be the same things from your past, or they may be different things, but there are certainly things. And your job is to listen to your heart and find what makes it sing again. Ok…maybe just hum a little at first.

So take a drive to the mountains. Or go to the ocean. Or sit in the woods. Whatever it is--do it. Amy made reference to an amazing little book she wrote to our children called *I Hope You Eat Chocolate!* The purpose of that book was to tell our children (and grandchildren) that we never want them to stop being kids. I want that for you as well. After all, it is God's will for your life...

> *"Thy kingdom come, thy will be done,*
> *On earth, as it is in heaven."*

FAITH INTERRUPTED

18
Dirty Hands and Skinned Knees

Journal Excerpt:

Like a newborn child opening his eyes to the world, my faith was born with hope and innocence. It was nurtured and loved as it explored this new world. A fairytale childhood was full of adventure and laughter and freedom. Through the years my faith grew strong until it could guide me through the most difficult of times. It met challenges with strength. It faced questions with confidence. Years and years together had given us the familiarity of a pair in their golden years, walking hand in hand.

But, it was a journey that was not without

skinned knees and dirty hands...
...for that is the stuff life is made of.

To truly live I abandoned the safety of home and ventured into the unknown.

I got knocked down; I got hurt.

As I found others along the way, I dug my hands into the dirt with them...and got messy.

But I know that when I walk the final few miles of my life, I will find the fondest memories are not of the hope and innocence that were birthed. No, the mind will reach back with longing to the depths of fearless passion, the grit it took to move beyond destruction, and halting bravery in the face of tremendous fear.

These will be my finest moments. These will be the memories I would die for.

FAITH INTERRUPTED

These rough and weathered hands will trigger memories one day.

The scars will tell their own story.

So, I choose to feel the depths of all that this life brings to me.

I will allow my faith to get messy.

I will not withdraw from the pain of skinned knees and dirty hands!

FAITH INTERRUPTED

Amy's Thoughts:

2 Corinthians 4:6-9 says that God *"made his light shine in our hearts to give us the light of the knowledge of the glory of God in the face of Christ. But we have this treasure in jars of clay to show that this all-surpassing power is from God and not from us. We are hard pressed on every side, but not crushed; perplexed, but not in despair; persecuted, but not abandoned; struck down, but not destroyed."*

When we were kids, we loved our scars, didn't we? Do you remember showing Grandma your skinned knee? You would proudly tell the story of how you jumped off the swing when you were at the highest point or slid into home base to score for your team. Chelsea still gives a dramatic account of her brother, Josh, hitting her in the head with a tool box! Then there was the time she fell through the floor in a house we were remodeling. Josh fell and broke his front tooth…a couple times. I sat on a cactus once…

Life is messy at best, tragic at its worst. I do hate the pain and struggles I have gone through, but now they have become my badge of courage. They are the story — the adventure — of walking with God. They are the demonstration of my rough, fragile jar of clay holding the very power of God within me!

FAITH INTERRUPTED

Dr. Dave's Counsel:

Retrospection is a powerful thing. It's the wisdom that only years can bring to a person. I believe it's why God really, really, really wants us to honor and embrace our elders. They have a perspective that can only come from looking back. There comes a point in healing, perhaps the final point, when we are able to look at our devastation from a painless viewpoint. That can take years, or decades. But it can happen. It does happen. And for you it will happen. I know it did for me.

> *Become the catalyst for change in someone else's reality*

Amy mentioned the power of scars. Where there is a scar, there is a story. I have an 11-inch scar on my abdomen--there's a medical story there. I have a quarter-sized scar on my arm--there's another medical story there. I have a pea-sized scar on my right hand--there's a story about a door there. I have a crooked nose--there's a college basketball story there. I have an oddly shaped left-ankle and am supposed to walk with a distinct limp (which thankfully I do not) --there are a

FAITH INTERRUPTED

series of basketball stories there. Some are funny. Some are scary. But each one of them has a story. These are visual scars, ones that can be seen. Our hearts have scars too. Normally these scars can't be seen by others. But they are real nonetheless, and frequently much more severe than the ones on our skin.

Retrospection provides the distance, the wisdom and the courage to understand the story of our heart-scars, and to make sense of them. As that understanding comes to us, it eases any lingering doubt, and eventually takes shape in our minds as a story. Retrospection then allows us to see that narrative in a new way, and fashions it into powerful experience that can be shared with others…and indeed should be.

This, my friends, is the place of ultimate healing.

When your *dirty hands and skinned knees* become the stuff of legend.

When you take your trauma-bull by the horns, and shape it into something that becomes a benefit to others.

When you share your struggle to free others from the same or to keep them from ever experiencing it in the first place.

Yes, this is what God ultimately intends for us in our devastation: **to become the catalyst for change in**

FAITH INTERRUPTED

someone else's reality.

Think of it this way: how much of the Bible is about people living their lives the right way? Very little. In fact, in those cases where people did follow God, they were often killed. And in the only case where an individual was perfect, He was crucified for His efforts. You see, God's message is always about redemption. It's about coming back from what stopped you. It's about trying again...and maybe even again...in order to help those who come behind you.

Let me ask you this...wouldn't you love there to be some EPIC, higher purpose to your season of devastation? Wouldn't it have made it much easier to know that before it all went down, or even during the event? God didn't do that for me. You see, He wanted me to experience the depth of the trauma, the fullness of the pain, so that I might one day consider it all in retrospection and try to help another traveler on the road.

But He eventually gives retrospection. I now look back and I see the good that came from it. Amy and I honestly rejoice that it happened. We see the benefits, we see things that we could not see at the time, and might not have believed if God has just spoken a word to us.

And so we find ourselves here now, 9 years later.

FAITH INTERRUPTED

Writing about it.
Speaking about it.
Sharing it with you, so that you can find your way as well.

So what is your legacy? What message will you leave behind from your life-altering situation? What lives will you change in light of it? Who will be forever benefited because of your journey? The answer to those questions lies entirely with you. It's time for you to mark the world with your experience, and to give it as a gift to others. Will you?

Conclusion

Journal Excerpt:

My faith was interrupted,
But not stolen away.
My life was devastated,
But the stuff of who I am cannot be destroyed.

It is my life,
And I choose to embrace it—all of it.

And because of that,...I am truly alive!

In Mark 5:34, Jesus said to her,

> *"Daughter, your faith has healed you.*
> *Go in peace and be freed from your suffering!"*

About the Authors

Dr. Dave and Amy DeMasters met in college and have been crazy-in-love partners for over 30 years, with two incredible children, Josh and Chelsea. They have served in full time ministry for over 20 years as senior pastors and church planters (and every other possible job!). **Amy** is the author of the inspirational book, *I Hope You Eat Chocolate!* She graduated from Bible College with an education degree and later earned her MBA and HR Management degrees. She speaks and writes on issues of faith and family.

Dave holds a Doctor of Ministry degree in Christian Counseling, and has an M.Div., MBA and Masters in Organizational Psychology. He is an engaging and entertaining public speaker, pastoral counselor, personal coach, and organizational consultant working throughout the country with individuals and organizations who desire to maximize their potential.

Other Works

I Hope You Eat Chocolate!

Available on Amazon.com

To Contact Authors

To Contact Dave & Amy, please use any of these media:

Website   www.FaithInterrupted.com
Facebook   FaithInterrupted/FACEBOOK
Email Dave Dr.Dave@FaithInterrupted.com
Email Amy   Amy@FaithInterrupted.com

www.ingramcontent.com/pod-product-compliance
Lightning Source LLC
Chambersburg PA
CBHW032050150426
43194CB00006B/473

9780692771983